# Do It Yourself Projects!

## Make Your Own
# Masks

# Anna-Marie D'Cruz

**PowerKiDS**
press.

New York

Published in 2009 by The Rosen Publishing Group Inc.
29 East 21st Street, New York, NY 10010

Copyright © 2009 Wayland/The Rosen Publishing Group, Inc.

First Edition

Senior Editor: Jennifer Schofield
Designer: Jason Billin
Project maker: Anna-Marie D'Cruz
Photographer: Chris Fairclough
Proofreader: Susie Brooks

Library of Congress Cataloging-in-Publication Data

D'Cruz, Anna-Marie.
  Make your own masks / Anna-Marie D'Cruz. — 1st ed.
    p. cm. — (Do it yourself projects)
  Includes index.
  ISBN 978-1-4358-2853-7 (library binding)
  ISBN 978-1-4358-2923-7 (paperback)
  ISBN 978-1-4358-2924-4 (6-pack)
  1. Mask making—Juvenile literature. 2. Recycling (Waste, etc.)—
  Juvenile literature. I. Title.
  TT898.D35 2009
  646.4'78—dc22
                                             2008033677

Manufactured in China

Acknowledgments
The Publishers would like to thank the following models:
Emel Augustin, Ammar Duffus, Teya Hutchison, and Robin Stevens.

Picture Credits:
All photography Chris Fairclough except page 4 top:
Archivo Iconografica, S.A./CORBIS; page 4 bottom: Reuters/
CORBIS; page 5 top: José T Poblete/CORBIS; page 9 top:
Dallas and John Heaton/Free Agents Limited/CORBIS

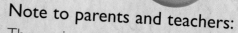

# Contents

# All about masks

A mask is something that covers all or part of the face, to hide it or to change its appearance. Masks have decorated faces throughout history— from Stone Age huntsmen, Egyptian mummies, and Greek actors, to today's modern performers.

## MASKS FROM LONG AGO

Masks were used as far back as the Stone Age, when huntsmen are believed to have disguised themselves as animals before stalking their prey. In Ancient Egypt, funeral masks were used to cover the face of the mummy, so that the dead person's soul would recognize the person's body in the afterlife. Some of these masks have been found in Egyptian tombs, such as King Tutankhamun's mask (see right).

## THEATER COSTUMES

Actors in the Ancient Greek and Roman theaters used masks to show emotion (feeling). In the Greek theater, all the characters were played by men, so those playing women wore masks of female characters. In the Italian comedy theater, *commedia dell'arte*, the lively characters were portrayed with the help of silly-looking masks. In Japanese Noh theater, the actors create the characters through body movement and masks (see left). Today, television and movie actors wear masks as part of the special effects that help make the characters more believable.

## FESTIVALS

Masks are worn during many festivals around the world. One of the most famous of these festivals is the Venice carnival. Like the New Orleans Mardi Gras, the carnival takes place before Lent and ends on Shrove Tuesday. People at the carnival wear traditional Venetian volto masks, masks of famous characters from the *commedia dell'arte*, such as Harlequin and Pierrot, or fantasy masks made especially for the carnival (see right).

## GET STARTED!

In this book, you can discover ways of making interesting masks from around the world. Try to use materials that you already have, either at home or at school. For example, for the cardboard in these projects, the backs of used-up notepads, art pads, and hardbacked envelopes are ideal. Reusing and recycling materials like this is good for the environment and it will save you money. The projects have all been made and decorated for this book, but do not worry if yours look a little different—just have fun making and wearing your masks. You could have a different face for each day of the week!

# Aztec skull

The Day of the Dead is an Aztec celebration that is still popular in Brazil and Mexico. The Aztecs believed that death is the beginning of a new stage of life, so the Day of the Dead is a happy time to celebrate people's lives on Earth. The skull is a popular symbol of this festival. Follow the steps to make your own skull mask.

## YOU WILL NEED

cream and white card
pencil
pair of scissors
glue
colored pencils
yarn
tape
hole punch
elastic cord

**1** Draw the shape shown on cream card so that it is big enough to cover your face. Cut it out.

**2** Use the information in the panel on the right to draw and cut out circles for the eyes. Make them large enough for you to see through. In the same way, cut out a triangular shape for your nose.

## DRAWING EYES

1. Close your eyes. Use the hand that you do not use to write with to point to your eyes.
2. Move your fingers onto the mask.
3. Use a pencil to mark where your fingers are and to draw eyes.
4. Cut out the eyes.

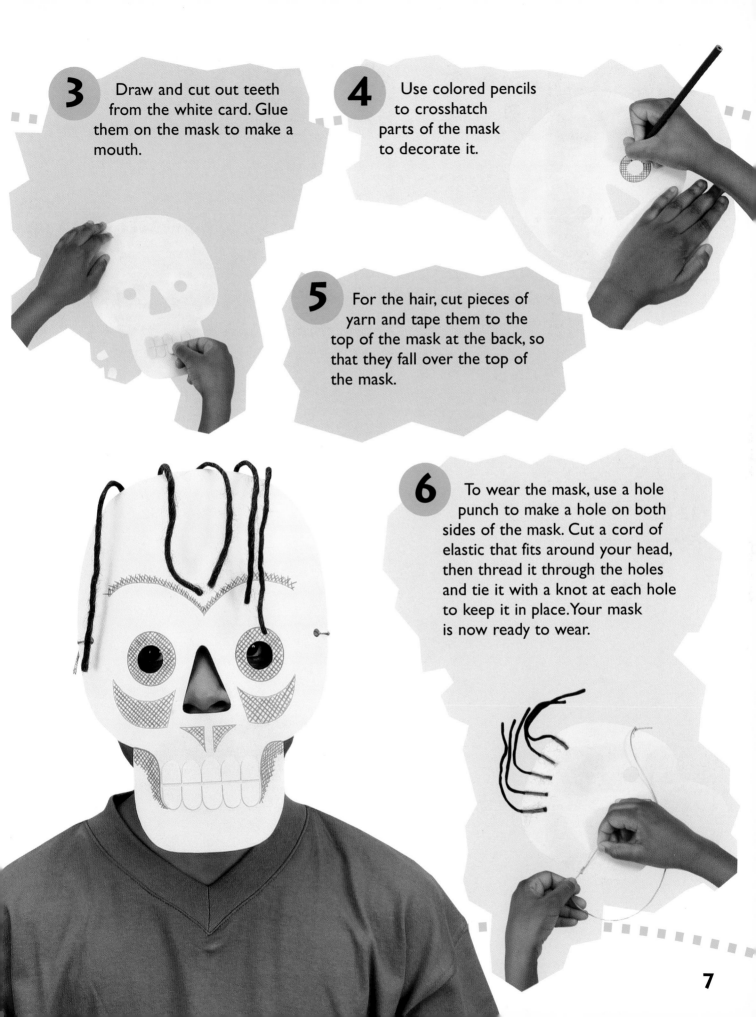

**3** Draw and cut out teeth from the white card. Glue them on the mask to make a mouth.

**4** Use colored pencils to crosshatch parts of the mask to decorate it.

**5** For the hair, cut pieces of yarn and tape them to the top of the mask at the back, so that they fall over the top of the mask.

**6** To wear the mask, use a hole punch to make a hole on both sides of the mask. Cut a cord of elastic that fits around your head, then thread it through the holes and tie it with a knot at each hole to keep it in place. Your mask is now ready to wear.

# Khon mask

Khon is a style of theater performed in Thailand, where the actors wear masks or crowns to represent animals, demons, and gods. The masks are brightly colored and often have gold crowns that are decorated with jewels. Use colored paints and lots of glitter to decorate your mask.

**YOU WILL NEED**

large sheet of colored card
pencil
pair of scissors
newspaper
colored paints
paintbrushes
glue
glitter
sequins
foil stars
gold pen
hole punch
elastic cord

**1** Copy the shape shown onto the card, making it big enough to cover your face. Cut it out.

**2** Follow the guide on page 6 to mark where the eyes need to be. Cut them out.

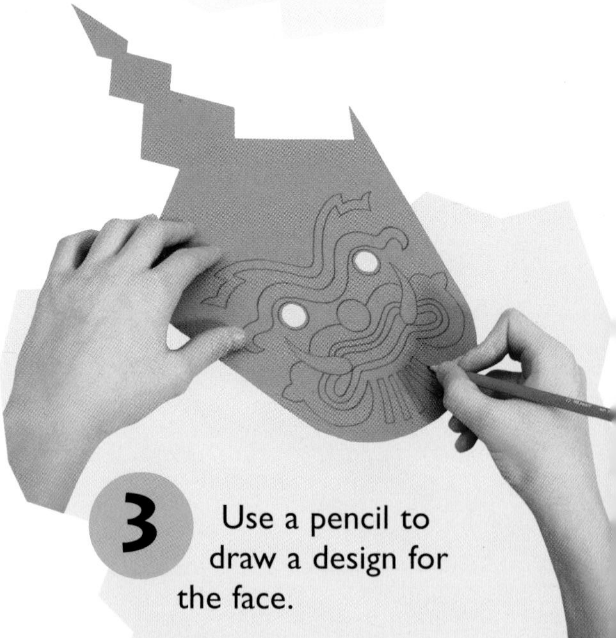

**3** Use a pencil to draw a design for the face.

**4** Cover your work surface with newspaper. Use different colored paints and a gold pen to decorate the face part of the mask. Allow the paint to dry.

**5** To decorate the crown, cover a small section of it with glue and sprinkle it with glitter. When the glue has dried, cover the next section with glue, adding more glitter, sequins, and foil stars.

# KHON THEATER

In Khon plays, the actors dance and do acrobatics. They cannot do any talking because their masks cover their mouths, so instead, other actors stand at the side of the stage to sing and tell the story.

**6** When the glue has dried, the mask is ready to try on. Use a hole punch to make a hole on both sides of the mask. Cut a cord of elastic that fits around your head, then thread it through the holes and tie it with a knot at each side to keep it in place.

# Carnival jester

Masks are made for carnivals around the world. The most famous carnivals take place in Venice, Italy, Rio de Janeiro, Brazil, and New Orleans. The jester is one of the most popular carnival masks. Follow the steps to make your own jester mask.

## YOU WILL NEED

large sheet of colored card
pencil
pair of scissors
colored paper
glue
stapler
rick rack
ruler
double-sided tape
hole punch
elastic cord

**1** Draw and cut out the shape shown from the card. Check that it fits across your face and over your nose, but does not cover your mouth. Cut out holes for your eyes, as shown on page 6.

**2** Cut out shapes from the colored paper to decorate the hat part of the mask. Staple rick rack around the edge of the eye part of the mask.

## MARDI GRAS

The New Orleans Mardi Gras (which means "Fat Tuesday" in French), is a time of parades and masked balls. The Mardi Gras lasts for a few weeks, but it ends on Shrove Tuesday— the day before Lent starts.

**3** To make the nose, fold a piece of card in half. Draw a triangle on the card that is wide enough at one end to fit on the nose of the mask. Cut out the nose.

**4** Make a small cut, about ½ in. (1cm) long, along the fold at the widest end of the triangle.

**5** Fold each side of the small cut upward to make tabs.

**6** Put double-sided tape on each tab to stick the nose to the mask.

**7** Use a hole punch to make a hole on both sides of the mask. Cut a cord of elastic that fits around your head, then thread it through the holes and tie it with a knot at each side to keep it in place. Put on the mask and get into the carnival spirit!

# Bwa sun mask

Crops need rain and sunshine to grow. In many countries, people depend on the rain and sunshine for all their food. This mask is worn by people in Burkina Faso in dance ceremonies to celebrate the farming season.

**YOU WILL NEED**

thin corrugated cardboard
pencil
plate
pair of scissors
masking tape
newspaper
craft glue
string
paints
paintbrushes
large popsicle stick

**1** Draw around a plate on the cardboard. Make sure the circle is large enough to cover your face. Cut it out. Use the guide on page 6 to cut out holes for the eyes.

**2** To make the nose, cut a triangle of card and bend it down the middle. Put strips of masking tape down each side to stick it to the mask.

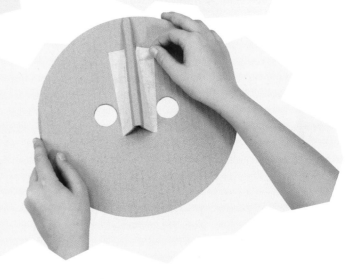

**3** Spread glue around one of the eyeholes. Circle string around the eyehole until you have gone around four or five times. Do the same with the other eyehole.

**4** To make a mouth, cut two circles from the cardboard, one smaller than the other. Glue the larger circle onto the mask where the mouth should be, and then glue the smaller circle on top of that.

**5** Cut triangles from the cardboard and glue them to the mask to make sun rays. Allow all the glue to dry.

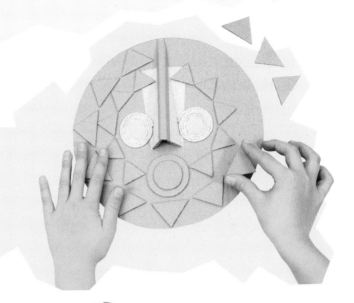

**6** Cover your work surface with newspaper. Paint the mask with bright-colored paints. When the paint is dry, tape a large popsicle stick to the bottom of the mask on the back. To wear the mask, hold it by the stick over your face.

# BURKINA FASO

Burkina Faso in Africa is one of the poorest countries in the world. Farming is important to the people of Burkina Faso, because most people work on farms for a living. If the crops do not grow, there will be no work or money.

# Kenyan giraffe

Lots of giraffes and other animals roam the plains of Kenya in Africa. This mask is simple to make and lots of fun. When you have mastered this animal mask, why not use the template on page 15 to make a lion mask?

**YOU WILL NEED**

large sheet of yellow card
pencil
pair of scissors
orange and brown paper
glue
stapler
elastic cord

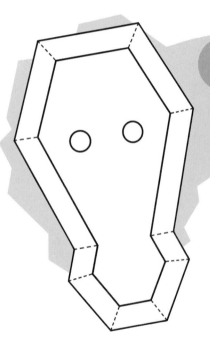

**1** Copy the shape shown on card, making sure the inner part is wide enough to cover your face. Cut out the shape. Cut out holes for the eyes, as shown on page 6.

**2** Cut out shapes from the orange and brown paper. Glue them onto the mask within the inner line, so that it looks like a giraffe's face.

**3** Using the template as a guide, make small cuts on the dotted lines, going up to the inner line. With the right side of the mask face down, fold up the edges. Overlap the cut edges and staple them together, but leave the area where the giraffe's nose meets the face unstapled.

**4** Cut two horn shapes from the yellow card. Add a small piece of brown paper to the top of each horn and cut a fringe into it. Fold the bottom edge of each horn in by ¾– 1¼ in. (2–3cm) to staple the horn to the top of the mask.

# ROARING FUN!

Use the templates below to make a lion mask.

**5** Cut two ears from the card. Gently bend over the top of the ear, and then the end of the ear by ¾– 1¼ in. (2–3cm). Staple the ears to the sides of the mask.

**6** Measure the elastic cord so that it can go around your head. Staple it to the sides of the mask. Your mask is now ready to wear.

# Egyptian mask

In Ancient Egypt, mummies wore masks made out of wood, stone, and precious metals such as gold. One of the most famous masks was worn by the Pharaoh Tutankhamun. Be a Pharaoh with your own Tutankhamun mask.

**1** Cut off the rim of half the paper plate. Cut out holes for the eyes, as shown on page 6.

**2** Use double-sided tape to stick the strips of fabric to the front of the plate, one to each side of where the rim has been trimmed off.

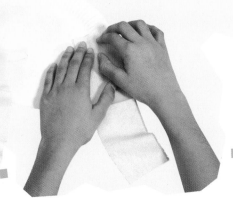

**3** Cover your work surface with newspaper. Turn the mask over and draw a face on the plate. Paint the plate and cloth, and allow to dry.

**4** To make a snake and vulture to decorate the mask, copy the shapes below on card. Cut them out and paint the details as shown. Paint the back of the vulture plain gold.

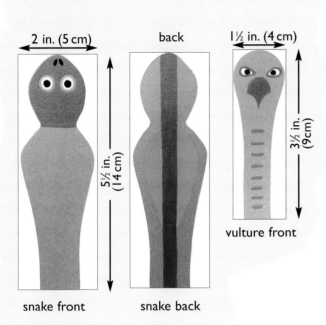

2 in. (5 cm)

back

1½ in. (4 cm)

5½ in. (14 cm)

3½ in. (9 cm)

snake front

snake back

vulture front

**5** When the paint is dry, gently bend the snake and vulture as shown, and staple them to the mask above the eyes.

**6** Decorate the popsicle stick in gold and blue, and when it is dry, tape it to the back of the mask at the bottom.

# TUTANKHAMUN

Tutankhamun became a Pharaoh when he was about nine years old. He died before he was 20. Following the tradition, he was buried with a golden mask and many treasures. His tomb was discovered in 1922 in Egypt's Valley of the Kings, more than 3,000 years after his death. Many of the Tutankhamun's treasures can be found in museums around the world.

# Greek Medusa

In Ancient Greek theaters, masks helped the actors to show sadness and happiness. They also helped the men to portray women and to be more than one person in the play. Why not wear your Medusa mask and perform in your own play?

**YOU WILL NEED**

card from cereal box
pencil
pair of scissors
stapler
newspaper
craft glue
green tissue paper
paints
paintbrushes
large popsicle stick
strong tape

**1** Cut the shape shown from the card. Cut holes for the eyes (see page 6) and mouth.

**2** Cut snake shapes from the card. Staple them around the top of the head to look like hair.

**3** Cover your work surface with newspaper. Twist strips of newspaper and stick them around the eyes and mouth. In the same way, add eyebrows and a nose to the mask. Scrunch up pieces of newspaper and glue them onto the snake shapes.

**4** Use glue to stick on strips of tissue paper, so that the whole mask is covered.

# MAD MEDUSA

There are many stories and myths about gods and heroes that come from the Ancient Greeks. Medusa was one of the mythological characters who had hair made of snakes. Medusa's stare would turn those people who looked at her to stone.

**5** When the glue is dry, paint the eyes, eyebrows, and mouth. Add eyes and mouths to the snakes, too. Allow to dry.

**6** Paint the popsicle stick green. When it is dry, use strong tape to stick it to the back of the mask. Your mask is now ready to wear!

# Viking mask

The Vikings were tough fighters, armed with spears, swords, axes, bows, and arrows. They protected themselves with round wooden shields and helmets made of metal or leather. Make this viking mask and be a ferocious Viking warrior.

## YOU WILL NEED
large balloon
shoe box
newspaper
craft glue
pair of scissors
thin corrugated cardboard
masking tape
kitchen foil
paints and paintbrush
stapler
strong elastic

**1** Blow up a balloon until it is the same size as your head. Knot the balloon. Rest the balloon on the bottom half of a shoe box.

**2** Cover your work surface with newspaper. Mix a small amount of water into some glue. Use this glue mixture to stick pieces of newspaper to just over one side of the balloon. Continue until you have built up about four layers. Allow to dry overnight.

**3** When the glue has dried, pop the balloon and remove it from the mask. Trim the edges of the mask. Work out where the eyes and mouth need to be and cut them out.

## VIKINGS IN ENGLAND

The Vikings were mainly farmers from Denmark, Norway, and Sweden. They traveled great distances in longboats to conquer and settle in other countries. In 793, the Vikings arrived in northeast England on the island of Lindisfarne, where they took over a monastery.

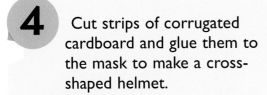

**4** Cut strips of corrugated cardboard and glue them to the mask to make a cross-shaped helmet.

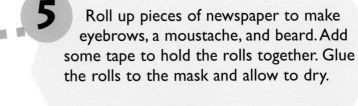

**5** Roll up pieces of newspaper to make eyebrows, a moustache, and beard. Add some tape to hold the rolls together. Glue the rolls to the mask and allow to dry.

**6** Glue lightly scrunched pieces of kitchen foil to the top half of the mask, covering the cardboard strips, too. Paint the face part of the mask and allow to dry.

**7** Staple strong elastic to the sides of the mask, long enough to go around your head and to keep the mask in place.

# Glossary

**acrobatics**

Jumping and balancing acts to entertain people.

**afterlife**

Life after death. The Ancient Egyptians believed that their soul continued living after they died.

**commedia dell'arte**

The Italian theater that was popular in the sixteenth to eighteenth centuries. Many of the plays featured the same characters, for example, Pierrot the clown.

**crops**

Plants, such as wheat, rice, and corn, that are grown for food.

**crosshatching**

Shading done with small crosses.

**jester**

A professional clown or joker. Jesters often wore a pointed hat with bells on the end.

**Lent**

The time from Ash Wednesday to Holy Saturday (the day before Easter). For Christians, Lent is a time for fasting (giving up certain foods) and prayer.

**masked ball**

A dance where everyone wears a mask to cover some part or all of their face.

**monastery**

The place where monks live.

**mummy**

A body that has been wrapped in oils and bandages to preserve it or stop it from decaying.

**myths**

Traditional stories.

**Pharaoh**

A ruler of Ancient Egypt.

**recycling**

To recycle something is to change it or treat it so that it can be used again. For example, the metal in soda cans can be recycled into other metal things.

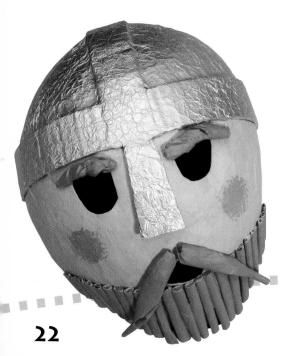

**reusing**
To use something again for a different purpose.

**Shrove (Fat) Tuesday**
The day before Ash Wednesday—the start of Lent. Because Lent is a time of fasting, people would use up their flour and eggs to make pancakes, which is why people eat pancakes on Shrove Tuesday.

**Stone Age**
The time, thousands of years ago, when weapons and tools were made out of stone.

**symbol**
A mark or object that is used to represent something. For example, a skull is popular symbol for the Day of the Dead festival.

**tabs**
Flaps or small pieces that stick out of something.

**tombs**
Places where people are buried.

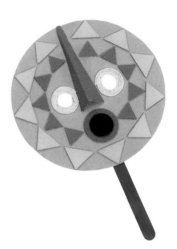

# FURTHER INFORMATION

## BOOKS TO READ

**DIY Kids**
by Ellen Lupton and Julia Lupton
(Princeton Architectural Press, 2007)

**Making Masks**
by Renee Schwarz
(Sagebrush, 2002)

## WEB SITES

Due to the changing nature of Internet links, PowerKids Press has developed an online list of Web sites related to the subject of this book. This site is updated regularly. Please use this link to access this list:
www.powerkidslinks.com/diyp/masks

# Index